whitestar˙kids

200
Q&As
About
DINOSAURS

Text by Cristina Banfi
Illustrations by Lorenzo Sabbatini

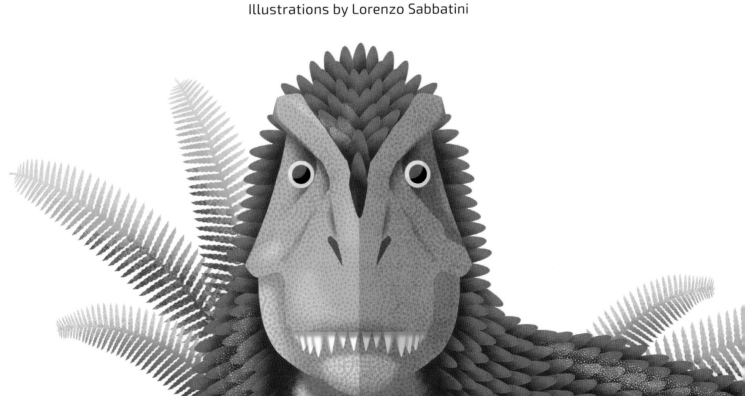

CONTENTS

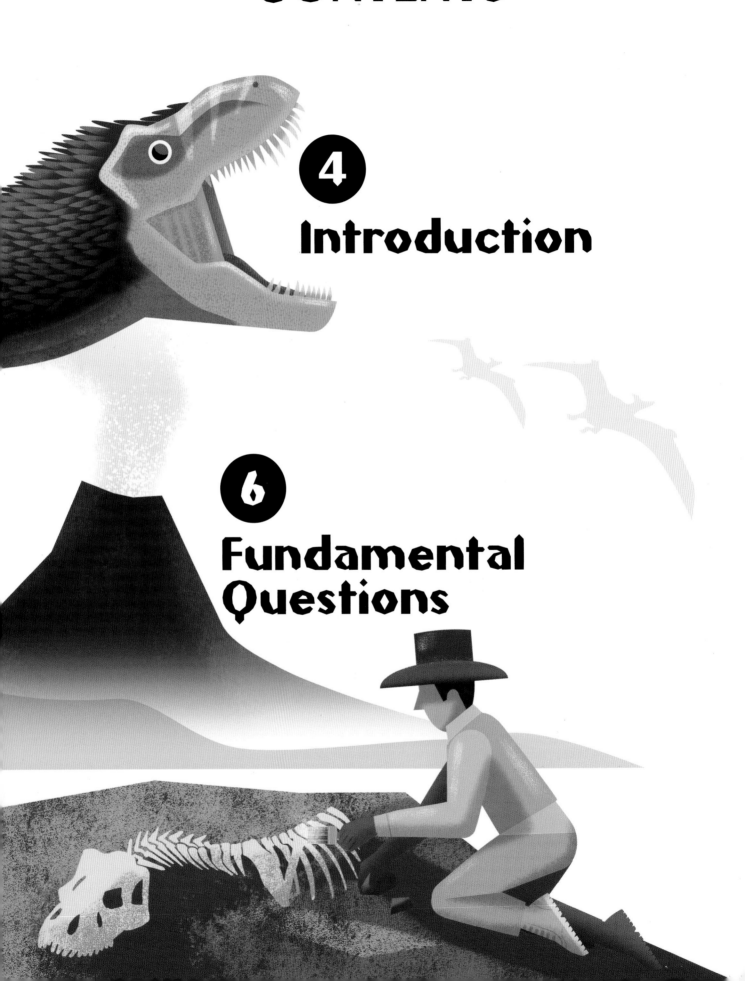

4 Introduction

6 Fundamental Questions

16 Carnivores

42 Herbivores

76 Flying Reptiles and Marine Reptiles

Introduction

Curiosity is what drives us to find out more about something, and asking questions is the best way to learn. Surely you have often asked for more information about dinosaurs, and you probably know some answers already.

After all, these **prehistoric reptiles** are well-known to just about everyone, although they lived millions of years ago. They populated our planet for an impressive 165 million years, in an interval of time that scientists call the **Mesozoic era**.

Then, about 66 million years ago, their story ended with a **mass extinction**; they disappeared forever, along with many other creatures of the sea and the sky. If we know anything about their existence today, millions of years later, it's only because their remains, petrified into fossils, have been found and studied.

The world of dinosaurs still holds many **secrets**, and numerous discoveries around the world provide new information every day. Let's discover some of them together and learn more about these frightening, peculiar, and incredibly fascinating animals.

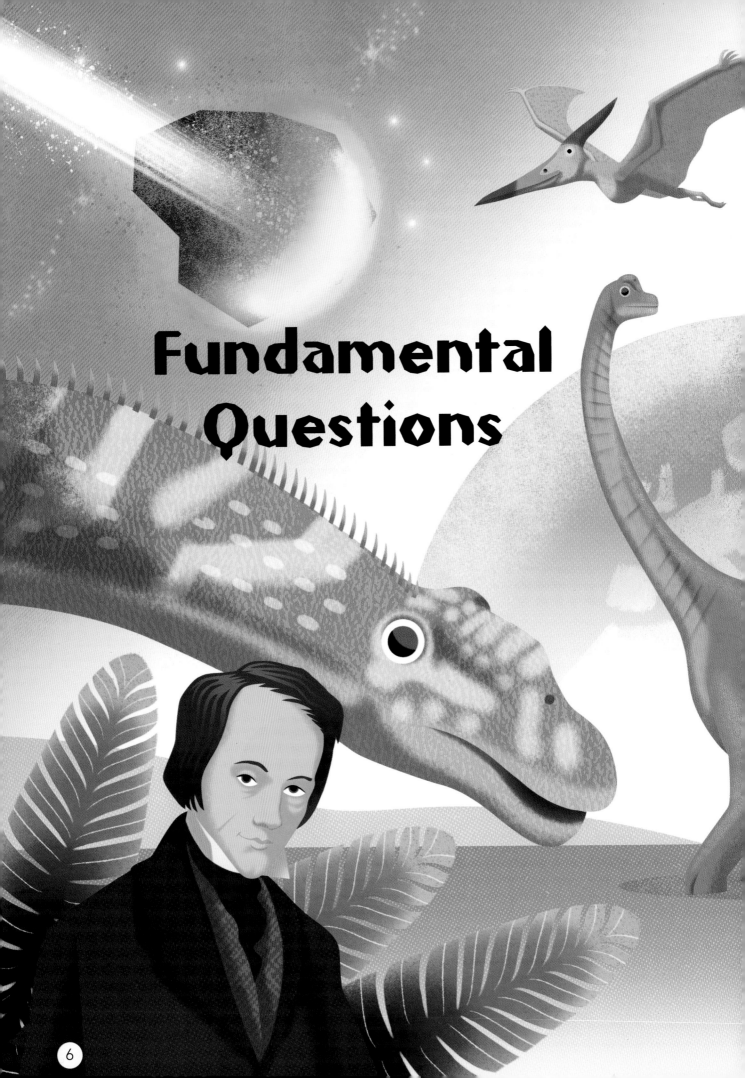

Fundamental Questions

Flipping through a book about dinosaurs, there are lots of questions we might ask. Why did they sometimes look so funny? What is that strange feature? Or, why did some have feathers and not nurse their young?

Or even, why didn't they pose a danger to early humans and why are there no more dinosaurs today?

Every answer will help you discover what life was like for these ancient lizards and why some scientists now think that they haven't really disappeared and that, in fact, they're much closer to us than you might think.

Why did dinosaurs go extinct?

Many scientists think that a huge meteorite hitting Earth rapidly changed the climate and environments all over the planet, making them suddenly unsuitable for dinosaurs.

Why are people who study fossils called "paleontologists"?

Paleo is a Greek word meaning "ancient," which is why it's used to describe those who study the remains of plants and animals that lived a long, long time ago.

Why couldn't prehistoric people hunt dinosaurs?

As a species, we fully became human a very long time after dinosaurs went extinct. Early humans may have hunted animals that are extinct today, such as mammoths or cave bears, but certainly no dinosaurs.

Why were some dinosaurs covered in feathers?

Dinosaurs were the first animals to have feathers. Feathers helped keep them warm, but also, if not actually to fly, they helped the animal elongate a jump by gliding. Some dinosaurs may have used them to impress a potential mate or frighten an opponent.

Why are dinosaur footprints important?

While not a body part, footprints can tell us a lot about a dinosaur's life: not only how it walked, but also whether it lived alone or in groups and how big it was.

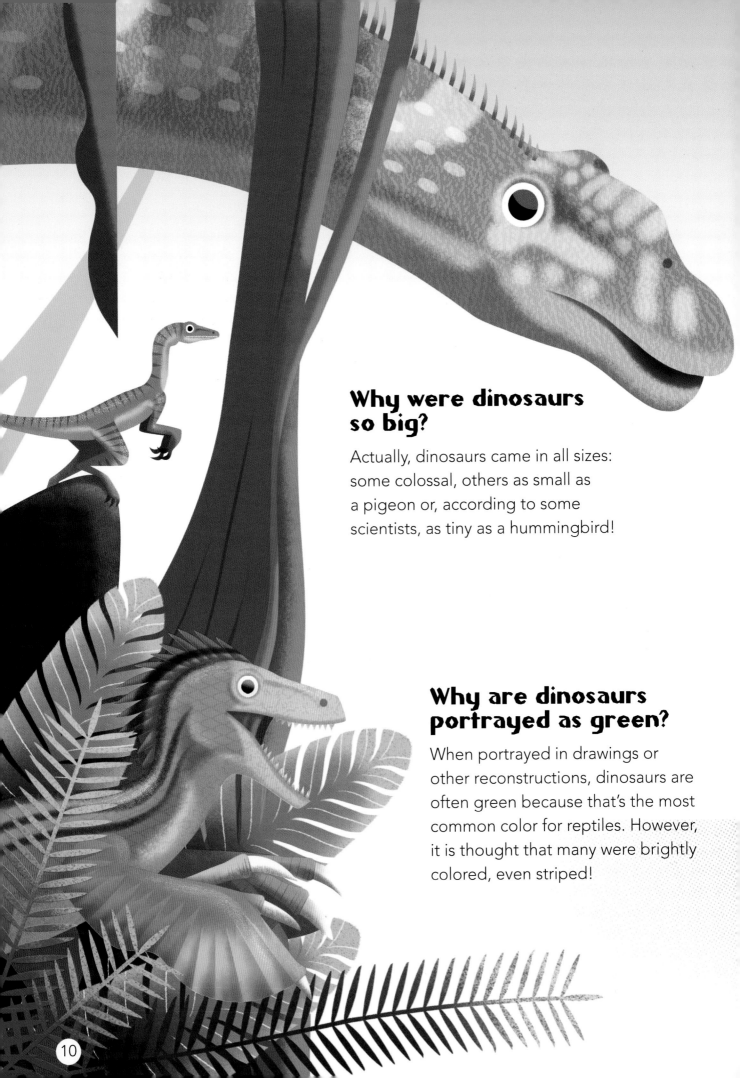

Why were dinosaurs so big?

Actually, dinosaurs came in all sizes: some colossal, others as small as a pigeon or, according to some scientists, as tiny as a hummingbird!

Why are dinosaurs portrayed as green?

When portrayed in drawings or other reconstructions, dinosaurs are often green because that's the most common color for reptiles. However, it is thought that many were brightly colored, even striped!

Why can we say that dinosaurs are still with us today?

Although dinosaurs went extinct, their descendants inhabit Earth today. Who? Birds! Which we can think of as small dinosaurs that learned to fly.

Why didn't dinosaurs nurse their young?

Some dinosaurs didn't tend to their young at all, while others raised them, nurturing and protecting them for a long time. Unlike mammals, however, mother dinosaurs didn't produce milk.

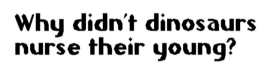

Why did dinosaurs lay eggs?

All dinosaurs laid eggs to reproduce. Generally, the eggs of carnivores were elongated, while those of herbivores were rounder.

Why is the Mesozoic era called the "Age of Reptiles"?

Throughout this long period of time, our planet was inhabited mainly by reptiles, including dinosaurs. They ruled supreme, having conquered all available environments, whether land, water, or air.

Why is it impossible to know what color eyes dinosaurs had?

Because dinosaurs lived millions of years ago, the dinosaur fossils we know today are mainly the hard parts of the bodies: bones, teeth, claws, and horns. Eyes cannot become fossils, so we'll never know what color they were.

Why are dinosaurs called that?

The term "dinosaur" was invented in 1842 by English paleontologist Richard Owen, who combined two Greek words, *deinos* and *sauros*, which, when combined, mean "terrible lizard."

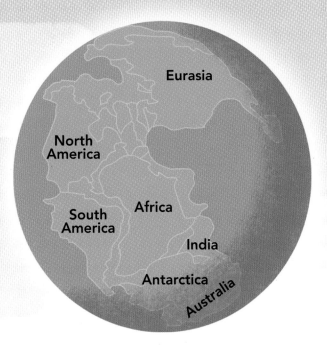

Why are dinosaur remains also found at the South Pole?

When dinosaurs lived, Earth's landmasses were united into a single continent called Pangaea. The region that is now Antarctica was once further north, and it wasn't covered by ice! Many plants and animals lived there, including dinosaurs.

Why didn't dinosaurs walk like reptiles do?

The main difference between dinosaurs and present-day reptiles is that dinosaurs' bodies were well above the ground when they walked, just like birds, thanks to straight legs that supported their weight.

Why are dinosaur remains found in rocks?

Bones and teeth may turn into fossils if the animal is covered in sand or mud after its death. Once a long time has passed, the sand hardens enough to become rock, which acts as a shell for the petrified remains.

Why didn't the earliest dinosaurs ever see flowers?

Plants with flowers appeared on Earth toward the end of the Age of Reptiles, that is, about 180 million years ago. Thus, only dinosaurs who lived at the end of the era could have enjoyed the beauty and fragrance of flowers.

Why did the mammal population grow only after dinosaurs went extinct?

The first mammals appeared together with dinosaurs, living side by side throughout the Mesozoic. But only after the extinction of almost all reptiles were mammals able to really evolve and spread, going on to inhabit all different habitats around the world.

Why are land animals today smaller than a lot of dinosaurs?

It's a matter of their physical conformation. The world's largest dinosaurs had bones with air sacs inside, which made them lighter, but they also had large lungs that provided oxygen to all the cells in their bodies.

Why do dinosaurs still have secrets to be discovered?

Paleontologists have not discovered all dinosaurs that once roamed Earth. Many are still waiting to be found. As new ones come to light, we learn more information about their now-vanished world.

Why do scientists think some dinosaurs were warm-blooded?

Reptiles today need to sit in the sun for a long time to warm up and be active. Some dinosaurs, however, were always very energetic, so, like mammals and birds, it's possible that they produced their own body heat.

Carnivores

Many dinosaurs were fast, cunning, and above all, armed with sharp teeth and claws. For nourishment, they ate other animals, which they caught by hunting. Crossing their path must have been really dangerous!

Some carnivores were truly huge and roamed alone, like tigers do today. Other, somewhat smaller dinosaurs preferred to live in packs, cooperating with those in their social group, like wolves. Generally, they all walked on two legs, keeping their tails high off the ground.

Why is T. rex called that?

The full name that paleontologists gave this dinosaur is Tyrannosaurus rex, meaning "king of the tyrant lizards." It's often shortened to T. rex, a rather fun nickname, don't you think?

Why were almost all carnivorous dinosaurs bipedal, that is, why did they walk on two legs?

Many carnivorous dinosaurs, especially the medium to large ones, were bipedal because they only used their hind legs to walk, leaving the front ones free for other things, such as firmly grasping prey.

Why couldn't carnivorous dinosaurs chew their food?

Dinosaurs only used their teeth to hold their prey and tear it into pieces. Those big bites were then swallowed whole, like sharks and crocodiles do today.

Why did T. rex have short arms?

Those tiny arms look ridiculous on such a large, ferocious animal. Exactly how they were used (or not used) is still unknown. Some paleontologists think they were a way for T. rex to lift itself off the ground.

Why is it thought that T. rex was not a predator, but a scavenger?

According to many researchers, since T. rex was so enormous, it couldn't possibly have ever run fast enough to chase and catch up with its prey, so it had to "make do" and eat the carcasses it came across.

Why couldn't T. rex and Tarbosaurus fight each other?

These two extra-large predators were very similar, and a fight between them would be very evenly matched. However, it is quite unlikely that they ever ran into each other because they lived in two very distant regions of Earth.

Why were the eyes of carnivorous dinosaurs so large?

Many carnivorous dinosaurs had large, forward-facing eyes to be able to better detect prey fleeing in front of them. That way, they wouldn't lose sight of their next meal.

Why did T. rex have large holes in its skull?

T. rex skulls, and the skulls of many other carnivorous dinosaurs, weren't compact but instead had openings called "fenestras." These holes helped lighten the weight of a huge head.

Why did T. rex have long, pointed teeth?

T. rex's teeth were even bigger than bananas and as sharp as daggers. This shape indicates that T. rex was a meat eater, meaning that it fed on other animals.

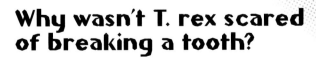

Why wasn't T. rex scared of breaking a tooth?

Even if one accidentally broke, T. rex ran no risk of being toothless because its teeth were continuously replaced by new, perfectly sharp ones.

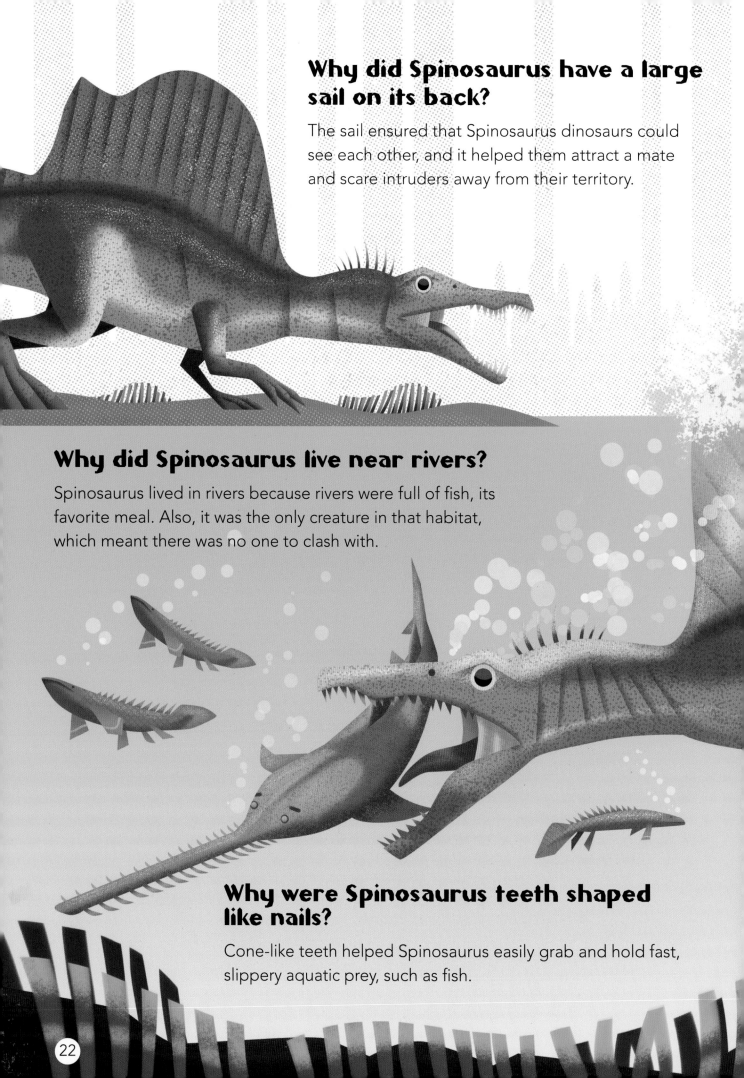

Why did Spinosaurus have a large sail on its back?

The sail ensured that Spinosaurus dinosaurs could see each other, and it helped them attract a mate and scare intruders away from their territory.

Why did Spinosaurus live near rivers?

Spinosaurus lived in rivers because rivers were full of fish, its favorite meal. Also, it was the only creature in that habitat, which meant there was no one to clash with.

Why were Spinosaurus teeth shaped like nails?

Cone-like teeth helped Spinosaurus easily grab and hold fast, slippery aquatic prey, such as fish.

Why did carnivorous dinosaurs have large mouths?

For many carnivores, their mouth was (and is) the only weapon for catching prey. For dinosaurs, their jaws were veritable bone-crushing machines that could tear off huge amounts of flesh with a single bite.

Why was the tail of Spinosaurus more than 3 feet (1 meter) high?

Spinosaurus's tall tail was shaped like a fin. It must have given the dinosaur a strong boost while swimming.

Why did Spinosaurus have webbed fingers?

Spinosaurus spent much of its time in rivers, where it was able to swim easily because of the taut skin between its toes. Its webbed feet resembled those of ducks today.

Why were Spinosaurus's nostrils on top of its snout and not at the very end?

Spinosaurus spent lots of time underwater. The position of its nostrils allowed it to remain almost completely submerged but also to breathe.

Why did Spinosaurus have a crocodile-like snout?

Its long snout, just like that of a crocodile, held sensory organs it needed to move through muddy river water, where eyes and sight would have been useless.

Why did Allosaurus have a short, muscular neck?

Allosaurus tore off pieces of meat by jerking its head backward, like eagles and other birds of prey do today. The short, strong neck gave it the strength it needed.

Why could Allosaurus open its mouth really, really wide?

Like the jaws of snakes, the jaws of Allosaurus were held together by elastic ligaments. This made its bite even more powerful.

Why couldn't Allosaurus fight T. rex?

Allosaurus lived many millions of years before T. rex. That's a very long time, even longer than the time when dinosaurs went extinct to the present.

Why did Velociraptor have a long talon on the second toe of each foot?

A single, elongated claw on each foot could have served, as in hawks today, to skewer prey and hold it so that it could not escape.

Why were several carnivorous dinosaurs also very fast?

For predatory dinosaurs, sprinting and speed were essential to catching their prey. They ran fast thanks to very muscular hind legs.

Why do experts think that Velociraptor had a good sense of smell?

Studying the skull of this dinosaur, paleontologists have found that the part of the brain corresponding to the sense of smell was particularly developed.

Why did Deinonychus hold its long talon upward as it ran?

For this dinosaur, its talon was indispensable for catching prey. If it broke, Deinonychus was in danger of starving to death. So, it held it up off the ground as it ran to keep it safe.

Why wasn't Deinonychus in danger of slipping when it ran?

When Deinonychus chased its prey, it probably zig-zagged to grab it. Its shorter toenails probably provided a good amount of grip on the ground.

Why is it thought that Velociraptor was nocturnal?

The eyes of these small predators were large enough to see even at night.

Why did Scansoriopteryx lean against tree trunks?

Thanks to its first toe, which was very strong and reversed, it would cling to tree trunks, somewhat like a woodpecker, to observe the land.

Why was one of Scansoriopteryx's fingers so long?

According to some scientists, this small dinosaur used the third finger of its long, skinny hand to collect insect larvae from holes in rocks or tree bark.

Why was Mei long given a Chinese name meaning "sleeping dragon"?

This small dinosaur was found in a curious position, with its head nestled under its wing. Perhaps a sandstorm or volcano ash caught it while it was sleeping and buried it.

Why is Oviraptor called that?

This name, meaning "egg thief," was given to it because the first specimen was found next to a nest full of eggs. It was thought to be attacking it. Later on, paleontologists discovered that the eggs were hers and that the Oviraptor was actually taking care of them.

Why did Ornithomimus have long feathers on its arms?

With feather-covered arms, Ornithomimus protected the eggs in its nests, providing the necessary warmth for the development of its young.

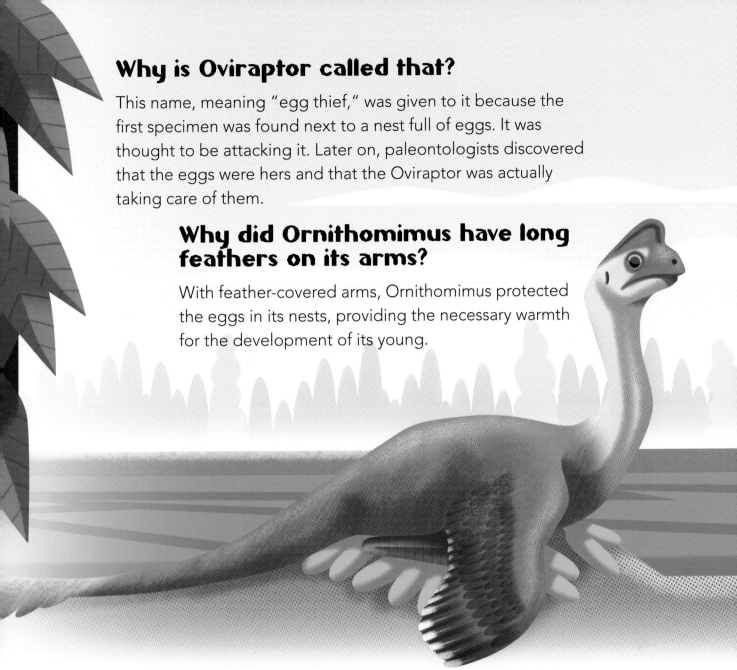

Why were Oviraptor eggs long and oval shaped?

These dinosaurs built nests very close together. The elongated eggs probably took up less space and were less likely to roll away.

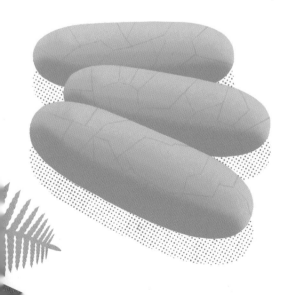

Why do paleontologists think Oviraptor eggs were colorful?

A shell color that is camouflaged with its surroundings would have protected the eggs during the mother's brief absences from the nest.

Why did Gallimimus have a beak?

This dinosaur probably had a varied diet: leaves, sprouts, and even small animals, such as insects and worms. Its beak made it easy to pick up a bit of everything.

Why did Gallimimus's beak look like a shovel?

This dinosaur had no teeth. It is thought that its wide beak filtered food particles directly from the water, just like ducks, which have gills in their beaks arranged in a comb pattern for this exact purpose.

Why did Gallimimus have hollow bones?

To be able to run at high speeds, Gallimimus had to be lightweight, despite its large size. As long as a crocodile and as tall as an ostrich, it did not weigh much because the bones of its skeleton were hollow, just like those of today's birds.

Why is Ornithomimus called that?

Ornithomimus means "bird imitator." These dinosaurs were in fact similar to today's flightless birds, such as ostriches: they had large legs, robust feet, long necks, and small heads, and were toothless.

Why did Struthiomimus have long, muscular back legs?

As with all ornithomimids, its strong point was running. It could reach top speeds while escaping from predators. It moved like ostriches do today; in fact, they probably looked a lot alike!

Why did Ornithomimus have very elongated feet?

The long, somewhat disproportionate feet of Ornithomimus were made of special bones, capable of dissipating its impact against the ground as it ran. A "normal" foot would have been easily broken.

Why were there smooth stones in the stomach of Sinornithomimus?

Having no teeth, this omnivorous dinosaur could not chew, so it turned its food to mush directly in its belly. The stones it ingested were moved by stomach muscles and functioned like millstones in a mill.

Why did Chirostenotes have small claws on its long feathered arms?

This dinosaur didn't have any teeth. It probably ate what it could easily find by digging into wood or in the dirt (things like insects and leaves), thanks to the claws on the long fingers of its hand.

Why did Pelecanimimus have a throat pouch?

Unlike other ornithomimids, Pelecanimimus mostly ate fish, which it caught in shallow water. To catch them faster, it would hold prey in a throat pouch, like pelicans do today.

Why was Deinocheirus named that?

Deinocheirus means "horrible hand" in ancient Greek. Indeed, its hands must have been fearsome: as long as a human arm, they had three fingers, each one with a huge claw.

Why isn't Deinocheirus believed to be ferocious?

Its long claws were blunt and may have served to pick up leaves or trap small fish instead of scratching other dinosaurs.

Why did some small carnivores hunt together?

Although it meant sharing a meal with others, smaller predators could catch animals even larger than themselves if they worked together.

Why is Troodon thought to have been very intelligent?

Troodon was not large in size (it was almost as big as a bicycle), but compared to other dinosaurs, it had a large brain, which certainly made it very clever.

Why did Dilophosaurus have two ridges on its head?

Its head was decorated with two long ridges made of bone, stretching from the snout to above the eyes. This strange headgear could have been used to get noticed by females.

Why is it believed that Dilophosaurus's ridges weren't used as a defensive weapon?

In the places where it lived, Dilophosaurus was a predator large enough to have no enemies. The ridges on its skull weren't very sturdy and would break if used violently against an opponent.

Why did Carnotaurus have small stud-like scales on its body?

The skin on its haunches was toughened by hard button-like scales, which probably helped protect those body parts, especially when clashing against its peers or other dinosaurs.

Why were the tails of bipedal dinosaurs long and thick?

The tails of dinosaurs that walked only on their hind legs were meant to help them stay balanced without falling forward, functioning as a counterweight to balance the animal's body.

Why are carnivorous dinosaurs also called "theropods"?

Researchers have gathered a large number of carnivorous dinosaurs in the theropod group, a word meaning "beast feet." All theropods had very sharp, powerful claws on their hands and feet.

Why was Albertosaurus named that?

This dinosaur, which was very similar to T. rex, owes its name to Alberta, the Canadian province where its fossilized bones were first found.

Why did Carnotaurus have two small horns on his head?

Its small horns were used when fighting other Carnotauruses. To support head-to-head impact, its neck muscles had to be very strong.

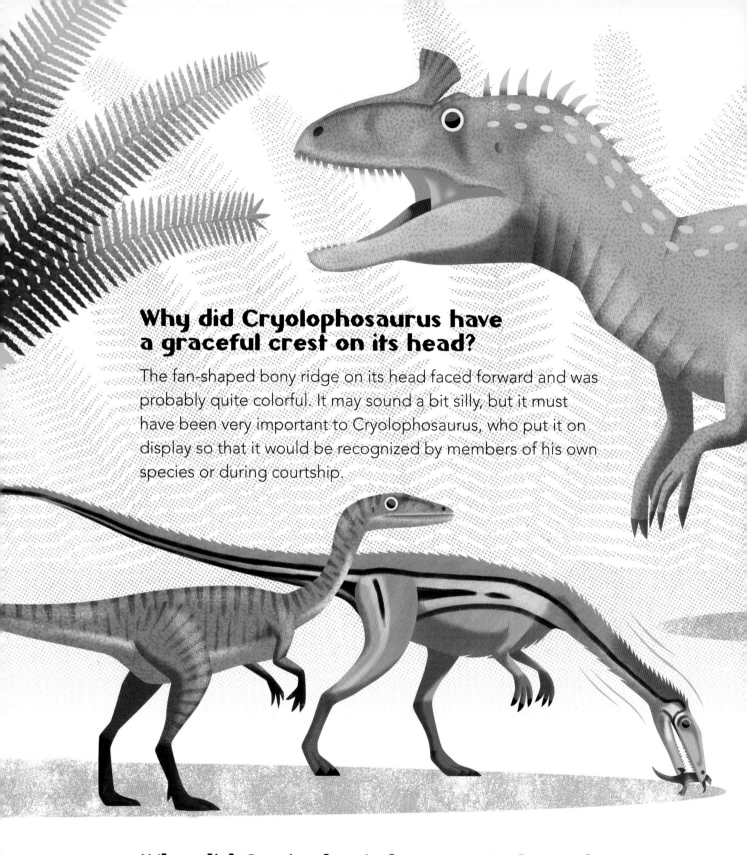

Why did Cryolophosaurus have a graceful crest on its head?

The fan-shaped bony ridge on its head faced forward and was probably quite colorful. It may sound a bit silly, but it must have been very important to Cryolophosaurus, who put it on display so that it would be recognized by members of his own species or during courtship.

Why did Coelophysis have an S-shaped neck?

Coelophysis's neck was long and slender, and when at rest, it took on the shape of an S. From this position, it could be straightened in a flash, allowing Coelophysis to pick up small prey found on the ground in the blink of an eye.

Why is Cryolophosaurus called that?

Cryolophosaurus means "cold crested lizard." In fact, its fossilized bones have been found in the frozen tundra of Antarctica and are evidence that the continent was once covered not by ice, but by large forests.

Why did Epidexipteryx have such long tail feathers?

It had four very long, ribbon-shaped tail feathers. They helped it to look more charming in the eyes of a mate during mating season and scared rivals away.

Why don't we know what color Epidexipteryx was?

Experts know that the body of this animal was covered with feathers because their impressions have been found among its fossils. However, it's very hard to know what color they were, as almost no traces of their pigmentation have survived up to the present day.

Why did Yi qi have small sharp teeth on the tip of its snout?

Its small peg-shaped teeth were used to catch insects and spiders, which it probably chased by climbing along tree branches.

Why did Microraptor have four wings?

Its arms were covered with long feathers, but unlike those of birds, they were too small for flight. However, the wings on its rear limbs were used to support itself when flying.

Why did Yi qi have a long, thin "extra finger" on each hand?

The name of this small dinosaur, discovered in present-day China, means "strange wing," precisely because its wings, very similar to those of bats, were formed by a very long wrist bone that held the skin taut between the hand and the body.

Why is it thought that Mononykus hunted small animals at night?

Having small teeth, it could only eat small prey such as insects and lizards. Its large eyes, on the other hand, suggest that it could hunt under the cover of night, when it was cooler and there were fewer predators around.

Why did Mononykus have a single claw on its forearms?

This small dinosaur had short, stubby arms and a single long claw placed on the thumb. Such a large nail was perhaps used to pierce the nests of the insects it fed on.

Herbivores

Along with the carnivores, there was no shortage of herbivores, who, in fact, did not eat grass at all, but vegetables of all kinds. They generally lived in herds, and they were constantly on the move, looking for food.

They defended themselves from predators in various ways, such as running away or whipping them with their tails, which were often armed. Some also had horns and hard plates all over their bodies, which protected them like medieval armor.

Why is Brontosaurus called that?

The name "Brontosaurus" comes from ancient Greek and means "thunder lizard." Given its enormous size, we can really imagine the booming noise produced by its every step.

Why were Plateosaurus teeth so small and sharp?

When Plateosaurus closed its mouth, its upper teeth crossed with its lower teeth like scissor blades, a foolproof method of shredding leaves and twigs for good.

Why did Apatosaurus have a thin, whip-like tail?

Like many similar dinosaurs, Apatosaurus had an exceptionally long tail that got thinner toward the tip. Experts believe it was used to whip predators or to communicate with its peers from a distance.

Why did Plateosaurus have long fingers?

Plateosaurus used its hands to grab twigs and bring them to its mouth. Having very short arms, those long fingers were essential to reaching branches way up high.

Why were Plateosaurus's hind legs stronger than its front legs?

Its large hind legs could easily support the weight of the dinosaur when it stood on two feet to defend itself or to grab leaves from the treetops.

Why did Brachiosaurus have a nose on its forehead?

Wide nostrils opened on the dinosaur's head, protected by enlarged bones. This position prevented leaves from going up its nose as it ate.

Why did sauropods' stomachs need to be so large?

Their large stomachs let them ingest a lot of food in very little time. Digestion, on the other hand, like for today's cattle, could be a very long process.

Why were Brachiosaurus's legs as thick as columns?

Its size was impressive, and to support such a heavy body, it required large, straight, vertical legs.

Why did sauropods have such long necks?

Moving huge dinosaur bodies required a lot of energy. Instead, if they effortlessly moved only their neck, sauropods could stand still and also reach the leaves in all the trees around them.

Why did sauropods have fleshy pads on the bottom of their feet?

Like elephants, they walked on their toes, which, as they spread out, were cushioned by a fat pad, not visible from the outside. This pad helped support their body weight while walking.

Why did sauropods have large, strong nails on their hind feet?

According to experts, these nails were used to dig nests in the ground, somewhat like sea turtles do when they lay their eggs in the sand.

Why did sauropods bury their eggs?

Sauropods did not brood their eggs but buried them in warm sand or under piles of leaves, which kept them warm enough until they hatched.

Why did Diplodocus have pencil-shaped teeth?

Such strangely shaped teeth were perfect for tearing up leaves and needles from trees: arranged in a line, its teeth acted like a rake and made it possible for huge amounts of food to be picked up with a few mouthfuls.

Why did sauropods have to have such a powerful heart?

The largest sauropods had their head at least 26 feet (8 meters) above their heart, so to be able to pump blood up there, their heart had to be very powerful!

Why didn't sauropods, which were giant in size, lay equally large eggs?

According to paleontologists, very large eggs would have taken a long time to develop. During that phase, the eggs were more likely to break before hatching.

49

Why is Argentinosaurus considered a record-breaking dinosaur?

It's considered the largest animal that has ever walked on land. Experts believe it was as long as two school buses and weighed as much as 10 African elephants.

Why did Camarasaurus have holes in its neck bones?

Paleontologists think that these holes once held air pockets, which helped make its very long neck lighter, while at the same time ensuring it was strong and robust.

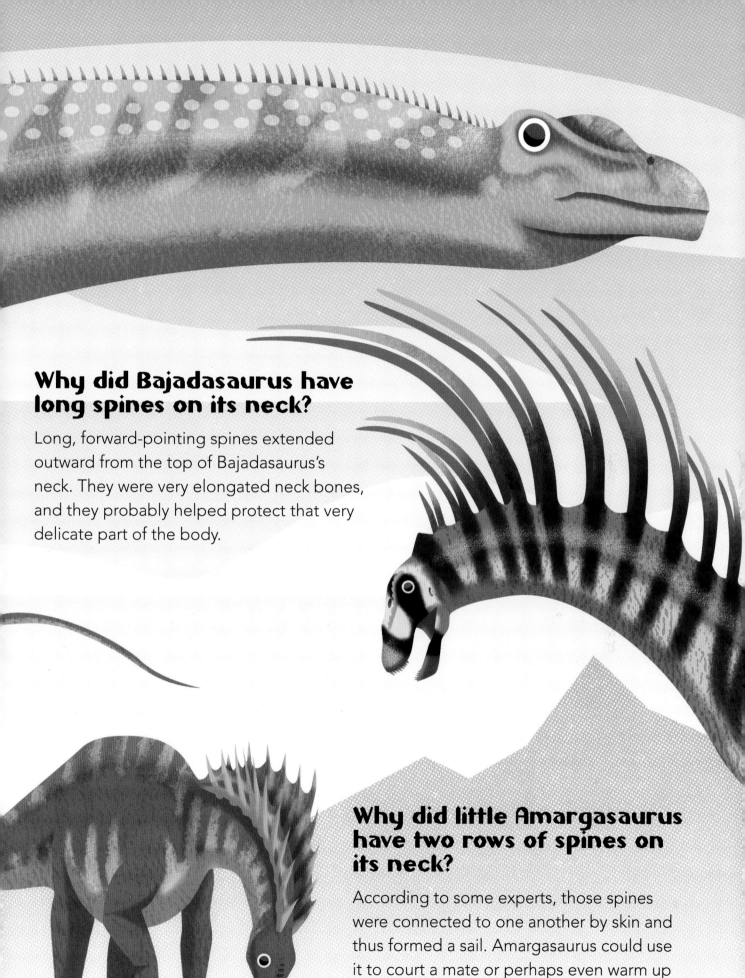

Why did Bajadasaurus have long spines on its neck?

Long, forward-pointing spines extended outward from the top of Bajadasaurus's neck. They were very elongated neck bones, and they probably helped protect that very delicate part of the body.

Why did little Amargasaurus have two rows of spines on its neck?

According to some experts, those spines were connected to one another by skin and thus formed a sail. Amargasaurus could use it to court a mate or perhaps even warm up faster in the sun's rays.

Why did Nigersaurus have an exceptionally wide snout?

The snout of this dinosaur resembled a vacuum cleaner. Wider than most, with hundreds of tiny needle-shaped teeth lined up in columns in its mouth, that muzzle was the perfect tool for grazing on small plants close to the ground.

Why did Brontomerus have such large thighs?

Brontomerus must have been a really strong kicker! Its particularly developed thigh muscles allowed it to kick very violently, both to defend himself and to fight against other males.

Why did Giraffatitan have longer front legs than hind legs?

Just like the giraffes from which it got its name, this dinosaur had very long front legs that helped it reach treetops that were as high as a four-story house, all without having to stand up on its hind legs.

Why did some sauropods swallow stones?

Some scientists think that the stones found in the stomachs of these dinosaurs were also a source of minerals for them. That includes calcium, which was probably scarce in their diet.

Why did Iguanodon walk on two and also four legs?

This dinosaur spent most of its time on four legs, but if something scared it, then it preferred to run on its hind legs only, making for a much faster getaway.

Why is Iguanodon called that?

The name "Iguanodon" means "iguana tooth." When its fossilized teeth were first found, researchers noted a striking resemblance to those of iguanas (aside from their size).

Why was Iguanodon's tail not only very long but also very stiff?

Just like its thumb spike, its tail was a defensive weapon used to ward off attacking predators. Moving it this way and that, Iguanodon prevented them from getting dangerously close.

Why did Iguanodon have a giant spike on its thumb?

The super thumb spike was used to bring twigs closer to its mouth and to defend itself when attacked.

Why was Maiasaura given a female name?

The name "Maiasaura" means "good mother." These dinosaurs lived in herds, and all adults built nests in the same place. The parents took great care of their young.

Why did hadrosaurs have pads on the bottom of their feet?

According to paleontologists, hadrosaurs' toes were invisible because they were grouped over a soft pad of flesh, similar to camels. That's probably because the foot had to support the weight of the body as the dinosaur migrated very long distances.

Why did many herbivorous dinosaurs have beaks?

When dinosaurs roamed Earth, the land was covered with plants with very hard leaves, such as conifers, tree ferns, and horsetails. In order to be able to eat them, a strong, very sharp beak was needed.

Why did Maiasaura young stay in their nest for such a long time?

Protected by their parents, who brought them food, young Maiasaura stayed in the nest until they were strong enough to fend for themselves.

Why are hadrosaurs called "duck-billed dinosaurs"?

All dinosaurs belonging to this group had an oddly shaped snout: it was elongated, then widened toward the mouth, similar to the beak of a duck.

Why did many hadrosaurs have crests on their heads?

The skull bones of many species were very long and hollow inside. Because air could be sucked in through the nostrils, those crests could have produced a very loud, distinct sound.

Why is it thought that hadrosaurs made noises?

Like many herbivores that roam Earth today, hadrosaurs lived in very large herds. In order to "talk" to their companions, they probably used the fastest mode of communication there was, namely sound.

Why did hadrosaurs migrate such long distances?

Because hadrosaurs ate such large quantities of plants and vegetables, they often went on very long journeys in search of food.

Why did hadrosaurs have multiple rows of teeth?

Some had more than 1,000 small teeth, including on the palate and cheeks, which acted similar to a cheese grater, crushing even the toughest leaves into bits.

Why did Ouranosaurus have a hump?

According to some experts, the hump must have been made of fat and, just as in camels, it was used for energy storage.

Why did Stegosaurus have big spikes on the tip of its tail?

The spikes on its tail could be used like a pickax to ward off large predators like Allosaurus. A well-landed blow could have done a lot of damage to the attacker!

Why didn't Scelidosaurus fear the teeth of carnivores?

Its body was protected by a kind of armor, with numerous rows of small, pointed bony "scutes" along its back and sides, from head to tail.

Why did Stegosaurus have flat bones lined up in a row on its back?

While we do know that it had two rows of flat bones on its back, we don't know exactly what they were for, besides protection and recognizing one another.

Why do some people say that Stegosaurus wasn't very smart?

Its head was pretty small compared to its body. So small that its brain couldn't have been bigger than a walnut!

Why did Edmontonia need such long intestines?

Digesting the hard leaves that this dinosaur fed on required a long passage through its intestines, which therefore had to be very lengthy.

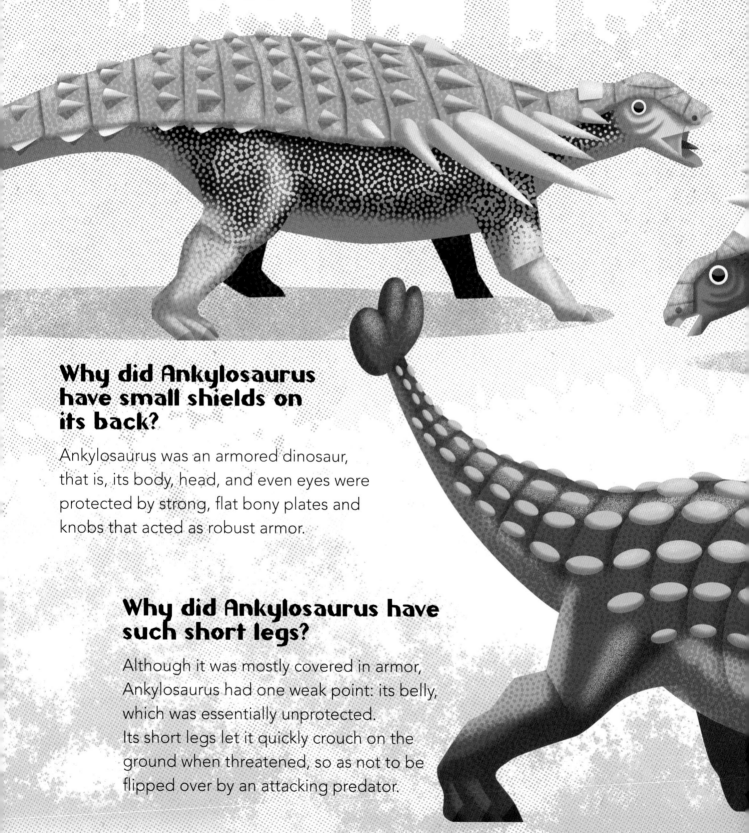

Why did Ankylosaurus have small shields on its back?

Ankylosaurus was an armored dinosaur, that is, its body, head, and even eyes were protected by strong, flat bony plates and knobs that acted as robust armor.

Why did Ankylosaurus have such short legs?

Although it was mostly covered in armor, Ankylosaurus had one weak point: its belly, which was essentially unprotected. Its short legs let it quickly crouch on the ground when threatened, so as not to be flipped over by an attacking predator.

Why did Edmontonia have big spikes on its shoulders?

According to some researchers, those long, forward-facing spikes could have been used by males in battles of strength with their peers, similar to deer antlers.

Why was Ankylosaurus feared even by large predators?

The tail of this massive dinosaur ended in a very heavy club made of bone. By striking attackers, the animal was able to defend itself.

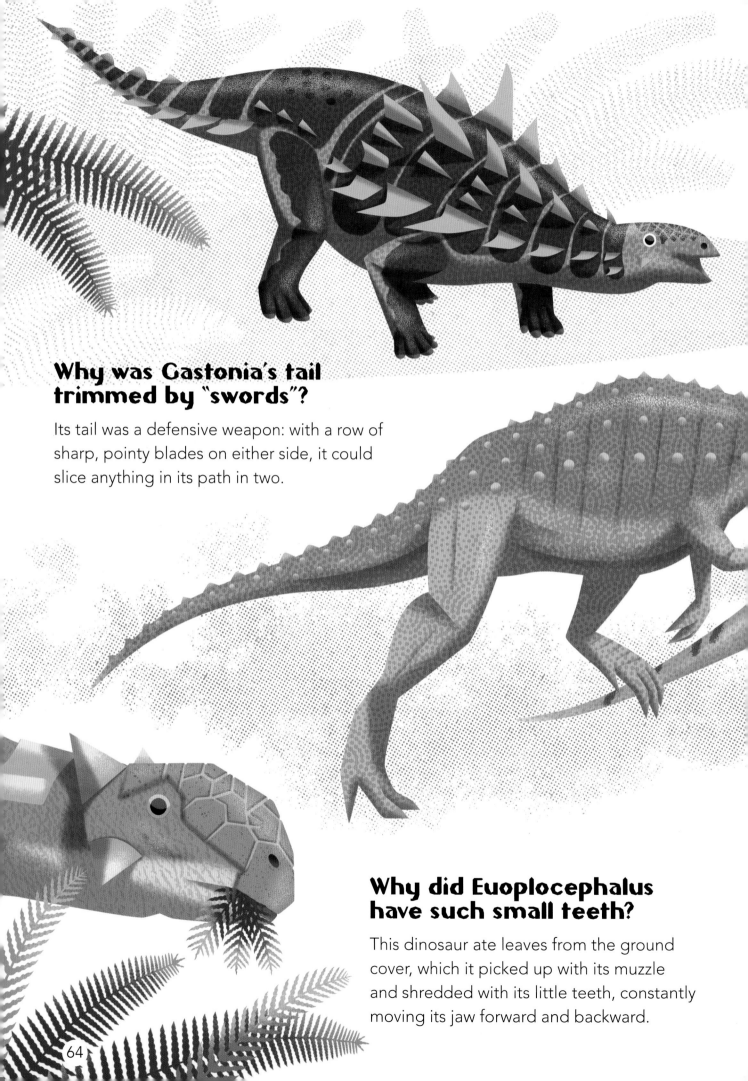

Why was Gastonia's tail trimmed by "swords"?

Its tail was a defensive weapon: with a row of sharp, pointy blades on either side, it could slice anything in its path in two.

Why did Euoplocephalus have such small teeth?

This dinosaur ate leaves from the ground cover, which it picked up with its muzzle and shredded with its little teeth, constantly moving its jaw forward and backward.

Why did Pachycephalosaurus have a "helmet" to protect its head?

Scientists think its helmet-like skull was a way to protect the brain, especially among males, who fought by butting heads to demonstrate their strength.

Why did Parasaurolophus have a long crest?

Its crest was formed by elongated skull bones. In males, the crest could reach almost 6.5 feet (2 meters) and was probably put on display to frighten opponents. What else might it have been used for? We talked about it on page 58—go read more about it!

Why did Therizinosaurus have fingernails as long as swords?

It's possible that its fearsome claws, which were over 3 feet (1 meter) long, were mainly used to bring leaf-covered branches closer to its mouth, a feast in just one bite, without having to move.

Why did Heterodontosaurus have canine-like teeth?

This dinosaur was herbivorous and ate leaves, so it's likely that its long, sharp canine-like tusks served only to defend itself from predators.

Why is it thought that Therizinosaurus lived in the forest?

Its mouth was shaped like a beak, so it was perfect for picking up leaves, which it chewed with small teeth placed in its cheeks. The forest must have been the ideal environment for it, full of lots of food.

Why didn't Therizinosaurus like open, treeless places?

Being large in size, Therizinosaurus moved very slowly. It therefore avoided going anywhere without trees, among which it could hide from large predators.

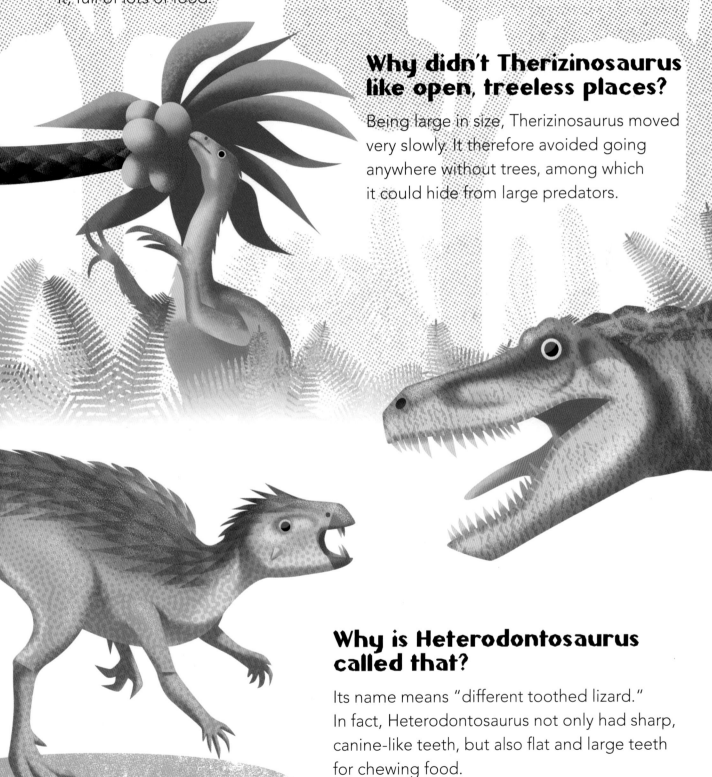

Why is Heterodontosaurus called that?

Its name means "different toothed lizard." In fact, Heterodontosaurus not only had sharp, canine-like teeth, but also flat and large teeth for chewing food.

Why are herbivorous dinosaurs with horns called "Ceratopsidae"?

The name of this family of dinosaurs comes from an ancient Greek word meaning "horn." The horns of these dinosaurs (some longer, others shorter, some with just one, others with many) are the feature shared by the entire group.

Why did Ceratopsidae have horns?

These huge herbivores were anything but gentle giants. Their long, pointed horns were their main weapon of defense against predators, but they were also used for fights with their peers.

Why were Triceratops's teeth always sharp?

Triceratops ate just about all types of leaves, even the hardest and toughest ones, and its teeth were easily worn down. For that very reason, it was constantly growing new ones.

Why did Triceratops hold tournaments with its peers?

Triceratops lived in groups: when mating season came, the males fought horn to horn to win a mate.

Why were Triceratops young raised by their parents for such a long time?

Triceratops babies were helpless because they lacked horns. For this reason, they relied on their parents, who could protect them from predators: the adults acted as a shield, forming a circle around their young.

Why did Triceratops have such a flashy "collar"?

Experts have come up with many theories over the years, but the most likely answer is that this "frill" made of flat bone was used to attract the attention of females.

Why did Styracosaurus also have long horns on the edge of its frill?

The large horns placed on the back of its frill couldn't spear enemies; instead, they served to make the dinosaur look bigger and stronger, which could thus scare off other dinosaurs with bad intentions.

Why did Diabloceratops sprout little horns on its cheeks?

The spikes that protruded from the sides of its head weren't actually horns, but skull bones. Some experts think the dinosaur might have used them to dig with its head in search of roots, which probably was one of its favorite foods.

Why did Chasmosaurus have two large openings in its frill?

The immense heart-shaped frill bone of this dinosaur had two large central openings. However, the openings were covered with skin (which was probably very colorful). Given their size, these openings perhaps only served to make the frill less heavy.

Why is Psittacosaurus called that?

"Psittacosaurus" means "parrot lizard." This dinosaur got its name because of its beak, which made it closely resemble a parrot.

Why did Psittacosaurus have long toes?

According to some paleontologists, this dinosaur had large feet for swimming in lakes and rivers; according to others, it used its long toes to dig in the ground in search of food or to build a burrow.

72

Why is it thought that, as an adult, Psittacosaurus walked only on two legs?

The fossils of this dinosaur make it clear that, after the first few years of life, its legs grew much faster than its arms, which then could no longer support the weight of the body.

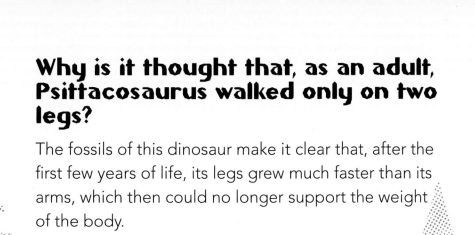

Why did herbivorous dinosaurs have eyes on the sides of their head?

Animals with eyes set on the sides of their head are usually prey. This eye position makes it possible to see a predator approaching from the right, left, and even from behind.

Why did large leaf-eating dinosaurs pass so much gas?

Plants are difficult to digest because they contain a very tough substance, cellulose, which takes a lot of time and the right bacteria to break down. As it's digested, a smelly waste product, namely methane gas, is formed.

Why did so many herbivorous dinosaurs live in herds?

Living in a group offered many advantages. For example, while everyone was busy eating, one member of the group (taking turns) could keep watch and sound the alarm in case of danger.

Why couldn't herbivorous dinosaurs eat grass?

For most of the time that dinosaurs roamed Earth, there was no grass. Meadows and plants with flowers began to enliven our planet only toward the end of the Mesozoic.

Flying Reptiles and Marine Reptiles

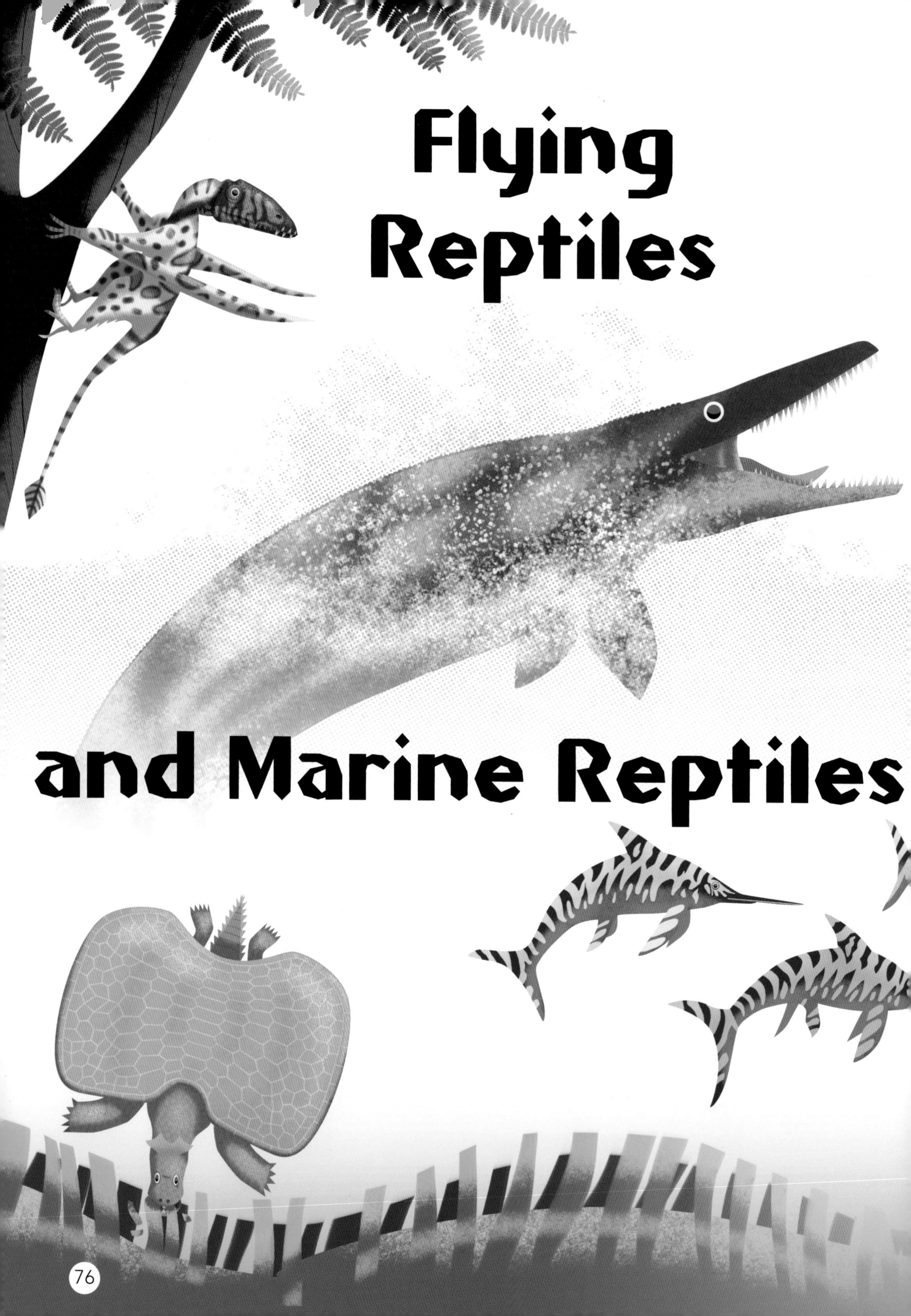

Pterosaurs weren't dinosaurs, but flying reptiles. And although they aren't related to birds either, they had a lot in common with them, living in the same environments and moving through the air.

Thanks to their large wings, they circled the prehistoric sky, perhaps chasing each other in flight and diving into the waves of the sea to catch their meals. Even the earliest ones had slender, lightweight bodies, and some had very bold, noticeable crests on their heads!

The oceans were ruled by marine reptiles that, although they aren't technically dinosaurs, are still really interesting!

During the Mesozoic era, they came in all sizes and shapes: there were ones with terrifying mouths like pliosaurs, but also less scary ones like ichthyosaurs, which made speed their strong point. All of them, however, swam thanks to feet that became fins. After all, they spent most of their time underwater!

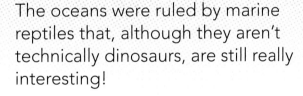

Why were the nostrils of marine reptiles found in front of their eyes?

Like dolphins and whales, ancient marine reptiles needed air to breathe. Thanks to nostrils on the top of their snouts, they could do so without having to poke their heads out of the water.

Why did marine reptiles have fins instead of legs?

These reptiles lived in seas, oceans, rivers, and lakes. Fins are the best appendages to do so, letting them swim quickly and easily through the water.

Why did plesiosaurs have such long necks?

Their necks could be longer than their body and tail combined! Perhaps that long neck was used to catch small fish swimming with their school or to search for prey in the sand on the seabed.

Why aren't prehistoric marine reptiles dinosaurs?

Prehistoric marine reptiles are often called "dinosaurs," but that isn't correct. They don't belong to the same family, and they have very different characteristics. For example, they were unable to walk on land!

Why did plesiosaurs have a short tail (relative to their neck)?

While their long neck was used to procure a meal, their short tail was useful for swimming. That's right, the tail was used as a rudder, to easily change direction in the water.

Why did many marine reptiles have a thin, very elongated mouth?

Marine reptiles with this type of snout fed on small, soft prey (e.g., small fish and squid), which they swallowed whole, in one gulp. That means they didn't need to chew them into small pieces.

Why did ichthyosaurs have a ring of bones around each eye?

Their eyes were protected in a way similar to a diver's mask. They could stand up to intense water pressure during deep dives.

Why did ichthyosaurs have so many fingers?

Based on their bones, ichthyosaurs had nine fingers per hand. That means that their limbs became wide flippers for swimming at great speeds.

Why was Shonisaurus so terrifying?

This reptile was as large as a whale and as fierce as a crocodile. Encountering it was dangerous for any inhabitant of the prehistoric seas!

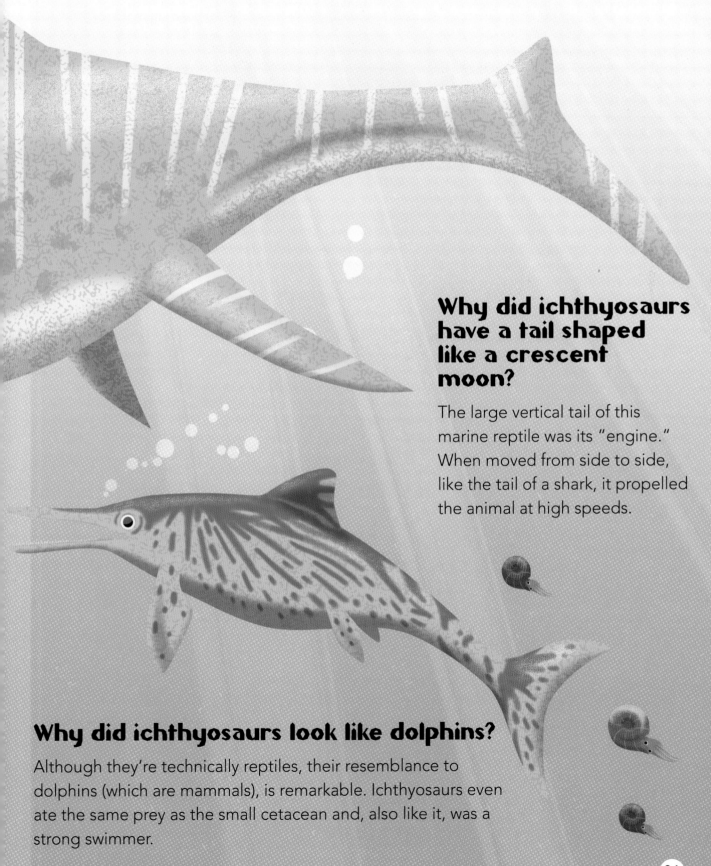

Why did ichthyosaurs have a tail shaped like a crescent moon?

The large vertical tail of this marine reptile was its "engine." When moved from side to side, like the tail of a shark, it propelled the animal at high speeds.

Why did ichthyosaurs look like dolphins?

Although they're technically reptiles, their resemblance to dolphins (which are mammals), is remarkable. Ichthyosaurs even ate the same prey as the small cetacean and, also like it, was a strong swimmer.

Why did mosasaurs have big, sharp teeth?

Sharp and firmly set in the mouth, mosasaur teeth allowed this skilled hunter to nab various prey "on the fly," including very large ones.

Why did mosasaurs have such a muscular tail?

Mosasaurs' hunting technique was to surprise their prey by attacking quickly. Their powerful tail muscles provided the force needed for a lightning-fast snap.

Why did Ophthalmosaurus have eyes the size of a Frisbee?

Its giant eyes let it explore the dark ocean depths far from the light of the sun.

Why did Nothosaurus have webbed feet?

Unlike many other marine reptiles, Nothosaurus didn't have true flippers, but webbed feet. This might mean that it could swim quickly and with agility in the sea but also get around on land.

Why did pliosaurs have larger back fins than front fins?

This rather short-tailed marine reptile got all of its swimming power from its muscular hind legs, which had to be very large and strong.

Why is Liopleurodon considered a record-breaking animal?

Its immense head occupied about one-fifth of its body, which meant its jaws were some of the largest in the watery depths. That made it one of the most fearsome hunters among all marine reptiles ever!

Why did Placodus have broad, flat teeth on the roof of its mouth?

This reptile ate shellfish such as prehistoric mussels and clams. In order to pry them out of their shells, it had to crush them against its palate.

Why did Eurhinosaurus have an elongated, sword-like mouth?

Such a strange upper jaw could perhaps have been used to stir up the mud on the seabed to flush out hidden critters and then devour them. Or, it could have been used to strike and stun its prey.

Why did Henodus have a flat shell?

Its solid, flat shell protected it from predators. To us, Henodus looks quite similar to a turtle, but really, the two animals aren't related at all.

Why didn't Henodus have teeth?

It actually had four: two on its palate and two on its lower jaw. All it really needed to eat was its stout beak, which it probably used to "scrape" seaweed along the seabed.

Why are pterosaurs called that?

All flying reptiles with skin wings that lived in the Mesozoic are called pterosaurs. The Greek word *pteron* means "wing," which is the defining characteristic they all share.

Why did pterosaurs have wings?

These reptiles conquered the sky millions of years before birds and bats. Their wings made it possible to fly.

Why did the wings of pterosaurs look like those of bats?

Like bat wings, their wings were made of skin stretched between the body, arm, and hand (though really, it's more of a very long fourth finger).

Why were pterosaurs so lightweight?

Their bones were hollow, meaning they didn't weigh very much. It's an important feature for an animal that had to lift itself off the ground!

Why did many pterosaurs have a crest?

According to many researchers, their crests must have been very colorful and probably were displayed to find and impress a mate.

Why haven't any fossilized pterosaur eggs been found?

Like a great many reptiles, they laid eggs to reproduce. It's likely that they buried those eggs in moist soil, and because their shells were soft and porous, the eggs didn't turn into fossils.

Why did pterosaurs have fingers on their wings?

In addition to a fourth finger that formed part of the wing (the "wingfinger"), they had three much smaller fingers. When the animal was on the ground, it folded its wings to the sides of its body and walked on all fours, thus also putting some weight on its fingers.

Why did Elanodactylus have a long neck?

This animal ate small aquatic animals, filtering them through the mud of wetlands and marshes. Having a long neck let it widen its feeding range without having to constantly move about.

Why were some pterosaurs "hairy"?

Some pterosaurs were covered with thin filaments, very similar to the body hair of mammals. It is likely that, just like hair, this layer helped keep the animal warm.

Why did pterosaurs need excellent eyesight?

Flying reptiles had to spend most of their time in the air, several feet above the ground. In order to be able to scout out food from that height, they had to rely on perfect vision.

Why did the teeth of Rhamphorhynchus stick out of its mouth?

Its favorite prey was small fish, which, thanks to these strange teeth, it could catch with ease, trapping them inside its mouth.

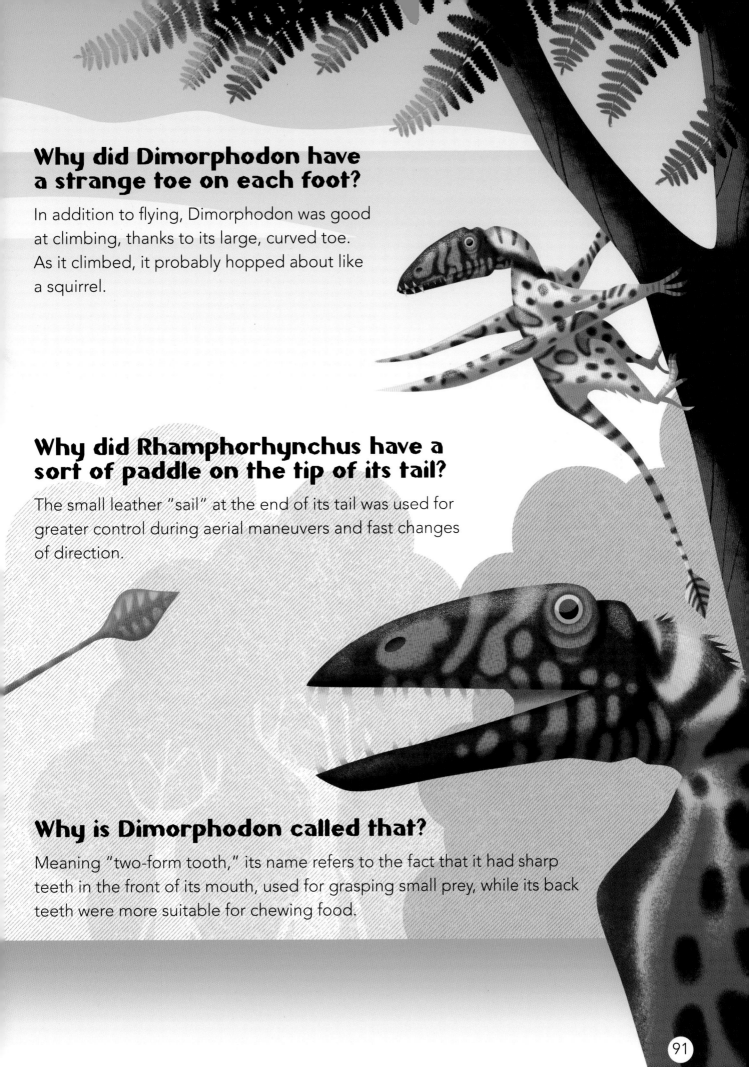

Why did Dimorphodon have a strange toe on each foot?

In addition to flying, Dimorphodon was good at climbing, thanks to its large, curved toe. As it climbed, it probably hopped about like a squirrel.

Why did Rhamphorhynchus have a sort of paddle on the tip of its tail?

The small leather "sail" at the end of its tail was used for greater control during aerial maneuvers and fast changes of direction.

Why is Dimorphodon called that?

Meaning "two-form tooth," its name refers to the fact that it had sharp teeth in the front of its mouth, used for grasping small prey, while its back teeth were more suitable for chewing food.

Why did Quetzalcoatlus have huge chest muscles?

To lift itself up into the air and fly, this giant pterosaur had to flap both of its giant wings at the same time. To do so, it needed immense strength, which only huge muscles could provide.

Why did Tupandactylus have a giant crest?

In pterosaurs, crests could be soft, stiff, narrow, thin, or even immense, like that of Tupandactylus. All of them, however, must have been very colorful, because they were used mainly to show off.

Why is it easy to distinguish male pterodactyls from females?

Paleontologists know that males had larger crests than females. Females had crests, too, but they were smaller and probably also less colorful.

Why didn't Quetzalcoatlus chew?

Its beak was very long and sharp, though completely toothless. However, it was so big that it could swallow small dinosaurs in one gulp.

Why is it thought that Tapejara ate fruit?

The shape of its strong, sturdy beak seems particularly well suited to crushing seeds, pine cones, and hard fruit shells.

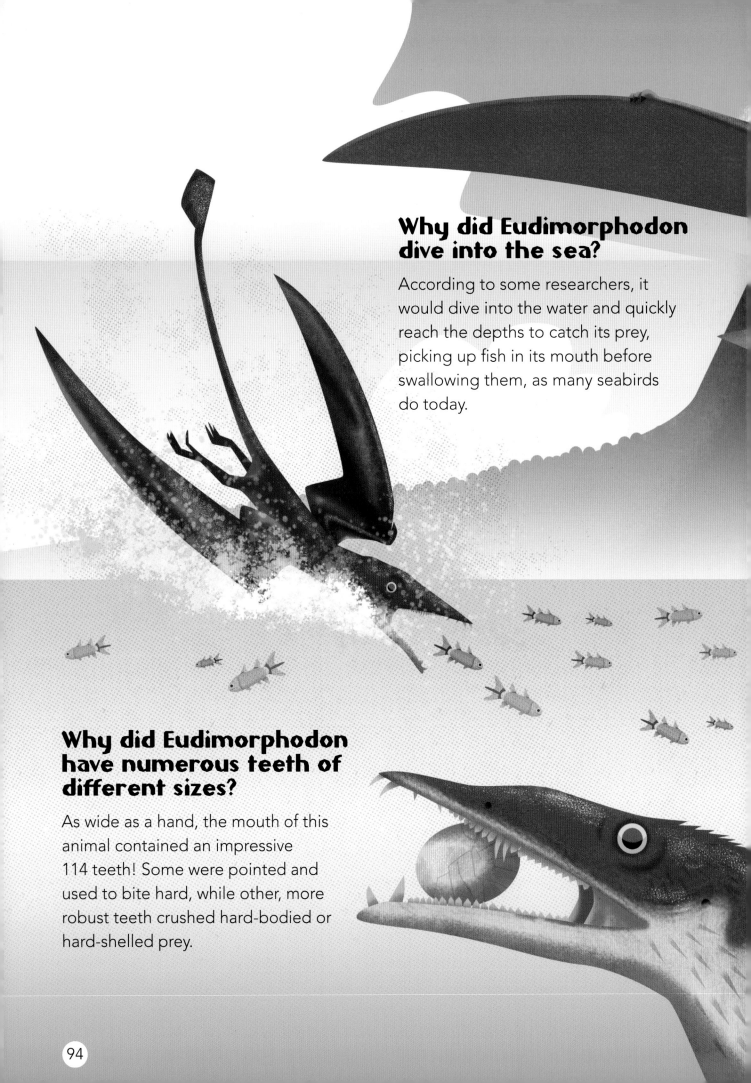

Why did Eudimorphodon dive into the sea?

According to some researchers, it would dive into the water and quickly reach the depths to catch its prey, picking up fish in its mouth before swallowing them, as many seabirds do today.

Why did Eudimorphodon have numerous teeth of different sizes?

As wide as a hand, the mouth of this animal contained an impressive 114 teeth! Some were pointed and used to bite hard, while other, more robust teeth crushed hard-bodied or hard-shelled prey.

Why did Pteranodon have extra large wings?

With such large wings, this giant of the sky could stay aloft for a long time without much effort, taking advantage of air currents. It probably also flew hundreds of miles away from the coast.

Why is Pteranodon called that?

Its name comes from ancient Greek and means "winged without teeth." In fact, it had no teeth and probably used the skin pouch under its beak, similar to that of pelicans, to fish.

ABOUT THE AUTHOR

With a degree in natural sciences from the University of Milan, Cristina Banfi has taught at several schools. She has been involved in science communication and education for more than 20 years and has been part of publishing projects in both scholastic and popular fields, particularly for children and young people. She has written various books for White Star Kids in recent years.

ABOUT THE ILLUSTRATOR

After studying industrial design, Lorenzo Sabbatini began working as an illustrator in the fields of publishing and marketing. He has been a member of AI, the Italian Illustrators Association, since 2006.

WS whitestar kids™ is a trademark of White Star s.r.l.

© 2023 White Star s.r.l.
Piazzale Luigi Cadorna, 6
20123 Milan, Italy
www.whitestar.it

Translation: Katherine Kirby
Editing: Abby Young

Second printing, January 2024

ISBN 978-88-544-2019-9
 2 3 4 5 6   28 27 26 25 24

Printed and manufactured in China by
Leo Paper Products, Kowloon Bay, Kowloon, Hong Kong